D1825411

CORIANDER

CORIANDER

southwater

This edition is published by Southwater

Distributed in the UK by
The Manning Partnership
251–253 London Road East
Batheaston
Bath BA1 7RL
UK
tel. (0044) 01225 852 727
fax (0044) 01225 852 852

Distributed in Australia by
Sandstone Publishing
Unit 1, 360 Norton Street
Leichhardt
New South Wales 2040
Australia
tel. (0061) 2 9560 7888
fax (0061) 2 9560 7488

Distributed in New Zealand by
Five Mile Press NZ
PO Box 33-1071
Takapuna
Auckland 9
New Zealand
tel. (0064) 9 4444 144
fax (0064) 9 4444 518

All rights reserved. No part of this publication may be reproduced, stored in a retrieval
system, or transmitted in any way or by any means, electronic, mechanical, photocopying,
recording or otherwise, without the prior written permission of the copyright holder.

Southwater is an imprint of Anness Publishing Limited
© 1997, 2000 Anness Publishing Limited

1 3 5 7 9 10 8 6 4 2

Publisher Joanna Lorenz
Senior Cookery Editor Linda Fraser
Project Editor Anne Hildyard
Designer Bill Mason
Illustrations Anna Koska

Photographers Karl Adamson, Edward Allwright, David Armstrong, Steve Baxter, James
Duncan, Michelle Garrett, Amanda Heywood, Patrick McLeavey
and Michael Michaels
Recipes Alex Barker, Roz Denny, Rafi Fernandez, Shirley Gill, Deh-Ta Hsiung, Shehzad
Husain, Liz Trigg and Steven Wheeler
Food for photography Elizabeth Wolf-Cohen, Carole Hanslip, Wendy Lee
and Annie Nichols
Stylists Madeleine Brehaut, Hilary Guy, Clare Hunt, Maria Kelly
and Blake Minton

For all recipes, quantities are given in both metric and imperial measures and, where
appropriate, measures are also given in standard cups and spoons. Follow one set, but not a
mixture, because they are not interchangeable.

Previously published as *Coriander: A Book of Recipes*

Contents

$\mathscr{I}$NTRODUCTION

$\mathscr{C}$oriander has always been highly esteemed in the East and in Mediterranean countries, where it has been used for thousands of years. Now, thanks to the influence of Thai and Indian restaurants and the popularity of Mexican food, Westerners have taken to it with a vengeance. The smell and flavour of fresh coriander is almost indescribable – you are either addicted to it, or would travel miles to avoid it. Coriander can be described as pungent and exotic, almost astringent, with a touch of citrus and cumin.

In America, it is known as *cilantro* (from the Spanish *culantro*). Confusingly, coriander is also known as Chinese parsley, although it bears about as much resemblance to parsley as mint.

Coriander is a wonderfully versatile plant. The leaves, stems, roots and seeds can all be used to create slightly different flavours.

In regions as diverse as India, China, South-East Asia, Latin America, Portugal and the Middle East, fresh coriander appears in all kinds of dishes either as a flavouring or garnish. It adds wonderful vibrancy and freshness to stews, curries, salads, soups, relishes, stir-fries, bean and chilli dishes. In Mexican and Asian

cooking, coriander, lime and chillies form a magical trinity which lifts seafood and salads to the realms of gastronomic euphoria.

Fresh coriander root is one of the key ingredients in Thai food, and gives it that unmistakable characteristic flavour. The root is pounded with garlic and black pepper to make a potent marinade for meat or fish, or it may be dried and ground and used as an ingredient in curry pastes.

Coriander seed is used in Indian and South-East Asian dishes where it adds an enticingly warm earthy flavour to curries, spice mixtures, marinades, relishes and fresh chutneys. It is also used in classic French marinated vegetable dishes.

The recipes in this book draw on exotic cuisines to enable you to experience the versatility of this plant. They begin with a mouthwatering selection of soups, starters and snacks, and then go on to fish and seafood dishes, with which fresh coriander is particularly delicious. The section on meat and poultry demonstrates the different flavours of the seed and the leaf. Anyone still in doubt will be won over by the final chapter with its inspiring selection of assertively flavoured vegetable and salad dishes.

Christine McFadden

Types of Coriander

Coriander Plant

The upper leaves of the plant are delicate and feathery; the lower leaves are broader and finely scalloped, similar in appearance to flat leaf parsley but with a flimsier texture. Use the lower leaves whole as a garnish, or chop a generous amount and add to dishes towards the end of cooking time for a wonderfully exotic flavour. Chopped leaves can also be used in salads, soups, curries, sauces and dips. Fresh coriander is also delicious in chutneys to accompany spicy dishes, and is a popular ingredient for fresh salsas.

Fresh Coriander Root

When you buy a bunch of fresh coriander leaves, check that the roots are still attached. They not only help keep the leaves fresher but are also a useful ingredient themselves. The roots should be washed and sliced, then chopped or pounded, and added to Thai-style meat or poultry curries, stir-fries and marinades, or added to other root vegetables in stews and casseroles.

Coriander Seed

Like the leaf, coriander seed has a distinctive, pungent, spicy, flavour. The colours of the seeds range from green to cream and brown. Use them whole, or crush as required. To bring out the warm, earthy flavour, dry-fry in a heavy-based pan for a few minutes before crushing.

Ground Coriander

Commercially ground coriander seed has a fragrant aroma and a pleasant taste, mild and sweet yet slightly pungent, similar to dried orange peel.

Coriander Paste

Made from fresh coriander leaves pounded with oil, salt and acetic acid, commercially produced coriander paste is a convenient substitute, but it lacks the vibrant flavour of the fresh leaf. It is sold in jars and can be stored in the fridge after opening for at least 12 months.

Coriander plant

Ground coriander

Coriander seed

Coriander leaves

Coriander paste

Fresh coriander root

ℬASIC 𝒯ECHNIQUES

REMOVING STALKS

Pinch off the upper leaves from the stalks, so that a minimum amount of stalk is still attached. Then pinch off the pair of leaves which grow further down the stalk. Discard the tough stalks. Wash the leaves and dry in a salad spinner, on kitchen paper or in a clean dish towel.

PURÉEING CORIANDER

Remove and discard any tough stalks from 75g/3oz fresh coriander, and roughly chop the leaves. Put in a blender with 30ml/2 tbsp each of lime juice and olive oil. Season to taste. Purée for 3 minutes, scraping the sides of the goblet frequently. Add more oil or lime juice if necessary.

FREEZING CORIANDER

Finely chop a generous amount of fresh coriander and freeze in ice cube trays. The frozen cubes can be added directly to cooked dishes. Don't use as a garnish – once defrosted, the texture deteriorates. To freeze the root, wash, wrap in foil and put in a sealed plastic bag.

BUYING FRESH CORIANDER

Choose robust, green, fresh-looking leaves. Avoid any that look limp, yellow or bruised as they will rapidly become slimy. Avoid bunches that have a large proportion of feathery upper leaves – they have probably bolted. Coriander will last longer if you buy it with the roots still attached. Chinese or Thai stores are a good source.

PREPARING CORIANDER SEEDS

Coriander seeds are the principal flavouring agent in many curries. For maximum flavour, use freshly toasted and ground seeds. Frying the ground seeds in oil before adding other ingredients releases even more flavour and gives the finished dish that characteristic "curry" taste.

DRY-FRYING SEEDS
To enhance the flavour, dry-fry the seeds without any oil in a small, heavy-based pan until you smell the aroma. Stir frequently and be careful not to let them burn.

GRINDING TOASTED SEEDS
Crush coriander seeds in a mortar with a pestle, or grind them to a powder using either a spice mill or an electric coffee grinder kept especially for the purpose.

CORIANDER SALSA

Skin, seed and dice 6 medium tomatoes. Halve, seed and finely chop 1 green chilli. Mix the tomatoes and chilli with 2 chopped spring onions, 10cm/4in piece cucumber, diced, 30ml/2 tbsp lemon juice, 60ml/4 tbsp chopped fresh coriander and salt and ground black pepper. Transfer to a serving bowl and chill before serving.

Serves 6

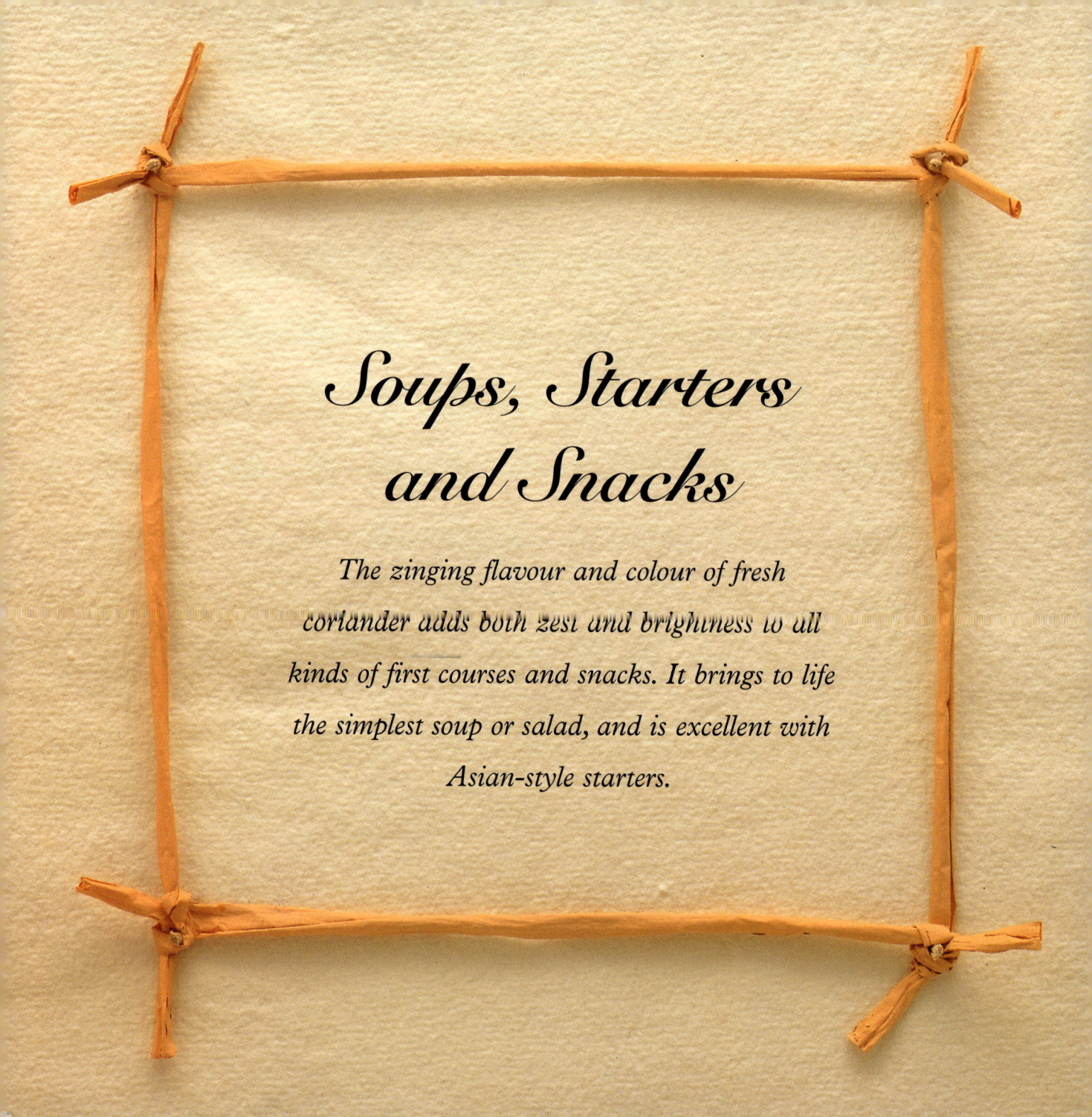

Soups, Starters and Snacks

The zinging flavour and colour of fresh coriander adds both zest and brightness to all kinds of first courses and snacks. It brings to life the simplest soup or salad, and is excellent with Asian-style starters.

CARROT AND CORIANDER SOUP

For maximum flavour, young carrots are best. Coriander accentuates their sweetness in this recipe.

Serves 5–6

15ml/1 tbsp sunflower oil
1 onion, chopped
675g/1½lb carrots, chopped
2–3 fresh coriander sprigs or
  5ml/1 tsp dried coriander
5ml/1 tsp grated lemon rind
30ml/2 tbsp lemon juice
900ml/1½ pints/3¾ cups
  chicken stock
salt and ground black pepper
chopped fresh coriander, to garnish

COOK'S TIP
This soup freezes well. After blending the mixture, cool it quickly, then pour it into a carton or similar container for freezing. Remember to allow a little headroom as the soup will expand on freezing.

Heat the oil in a large saucepan. Fry the onion over a gentle heat for 5 minutes, until softened but not coloured. Add the chopped carrots, coriander sprigs or dried coriander, lemon rind and juice. Stir well, then add the chicken stock with salt and pepper to taste.

Bring to the boil, lower the heat, cover and simmer for 15–20 minutes, occasionally checking that there is sufficient liquid. When the carrots are really tender, purée the mixture in a blender or food processor. Return to the pan, then check the seasoning.

Heat through again. Sprinkle with chopped coriander before serving.

Gazpacho with Coriander

Coriander gives this Californian cold soup its distinct and original flavour.

Serves 4

675g/1½lb ripe tomatoes

15ml/1 tbsp tomato ketchup

30ml/2 tbsp tomato purée

1.5ml/¼ tsp sugar

2.5ml/½ tsp salt

5ml/1 tsp ground black pepper

60ml/4 tbsp sherry or red
   wine vinegar

175ml/6fl oz/¾ cup olive oil

350ml/12fl oz/1½ cups tomato juice

1 large cucumber, about 225g/8oz,
   roughly chopped

½ green pepper, seeded and
   roughly chopped

½ red pepper, seeded and
   roughly chopped

2 spring onions, chopped

Tabasco sauce (optional)

60ml/4 tbsp chopped fresh coriander

croûtons, to garnish

Chop 1 tomato and set it aside. Peel the remaining tomatoes, remove the seeds and chop them roughly. Tip into a food processor or blender and pulse until just smooth, scraping the sides of the container occasionally.

Add the tomato ketchup, purée, sugar, salt, pepper, vinegar and oil and pulse 3–4 times to blend. Transfer to a large bowl. Stir in the tomato juice.

Place the cucumber and peppers in the food processor or blender and pulse until finely chopped; do not overmix.

Reserve about 30ml/2 tbsp of the chopped vegetables for the garnish; stir the remainder into the soup. Taste for seasoning. Mix in the chopped tomato and spring onions. Add a dash of Tabasco sauce if you like. Stir in half of the chopped coriander. Chill well.

To serve, ladle into bowls and sprinkle with the reserved chopped vegetables, croûtons and remaining coriander.

CAULIFLOWER AND CORIANDER SOUP

Light and tasty, this spicy coriander-flavoured soup makes a wonderfully warming first course, an appetizing quick meal or – when served chilled – a delicious summertime treat.

Serves 4–6

15ml/1 tbsp sunflower oil

1 large potato, peeled and diced

1 small cauliflower, chopped

1 onion, chopped

1 garlic clove, crushed

15ml/1 tbsp grated fresh root ginger

10ml/2 tsp ground turmeric

5ml/1 tsp cumin seeds

5ml/1 tsp black mustard seeds

10ml/2 tsp ground coriander

1 litre/1¾ pints/4 cups
    vegetable stock

300ml/½ pint/1¼ cups
    natural yogurt

salt and ground black pepper

fresh coriander or parsley, to garnish

Heat the oil in a large saucepan, add the potato, cauliflower and onion and toss to coat. Drizzle over 45ml/3 tbsp water. Heat until hot and bubbling, then cover and turn the heat down. Continue cooking the mixture for about 10 minutes.

Stir in the garlic, ginger, seeds and spices. Cook for 2 minutes more, stirring occasionally. Pour in the stock and add plenty of salt and pepper. Bring to the boil, then lower the heat, cover and simmer for about 20 minutes. Stir in the yogurt, adjust the seasoning and garnish with coriander or parsley. Serve at once.

CHICKEN STICKS WITH CORIANDER DIP

A refreshing coriander yogurt makes the perfect dipping sauce for these Tandoori-style chicken sticks.

Makes about 25

175ml/6fl oz/³/4 cup natural yogurt

5ml/1 tsp garam masala or
*   curry powder*

1.5ml/¹/4 tsp ground cumin

1.5ml/¹/4 tsp ground coriander

1.5ml/¹/4 tsp cayenne pepper

5ml/1 tsp tomato purée

1–2 garlic cloves, finely chopped

2.5cm/1in piece of fresh root ginger,
*   peeled and finely chopped*

grated rind and juice of ¹/2 lemon

30ml/2 tbsp chopped fresh coriander
*   or mint*

450g/1lb boneless, skinless
*   chicken breasts*

For the coriander dip

250ml/8fl oz/1 cup natural yogurt

30ml/2 tbsp whipping cream

¹/2 cucumber, peeled, seeded and
*   finely chopped*

30ml/2 tbsp chopped fresh coriander
*   or mint*

salt and ground black pepper

Prepare the coriander dip first. Combine all the ingredients in a bowl and season with salt and ground black pepper. Cover and chill until ready to serve.

Put the yogurt, spices, tomato purée, garlic, ginger, lemon rind and juice and herbs in a food processor or blender, and process until smooth. Pour into a shallow dish.

Freeze the chicken breasts for 5 minutes to firm them slightly, then slice them in half horizontally. Cut the slices into 2cm/³/4in strips and add to the marinade. Toss to coat well. Cover and chill for 6–8 hours or overnight.

Preheat the grill and line a baking sheet with foil. Using a slotted spoon, remove the chicken from the marinade and arrange the pieces in a single layer on the baking sheet. Scrunch up the chicken slightly so it makes wavy shapes. Grill for 4–5 minutes until brown and just cooked, turning once. Thread 1–2 pieces on to cocktail sticks or short skewers and serve with the coriander dip.

GRILLED GREEN MUSSELS WITH CORIANDER

Large green shelled mussels have a more distinctive flavour than the small black variety, and they are particularly delicious with this coriander crumb topping.

Serves 4

45ml/3 tbsp chopped fresh coriander

45ml/3 tbsp chopped fresh parsley

1 garlic clove, crushed

pinch of ground coriander

25g/1oz/2 tbsp butter, softened

25g/1oz/½ cup wholemeal
  breadcrumbs

ground black pepper

12 green mussels or 24 small mussels
  on the half-shell

chopped fresh coriander or parsley,
  to garnish

COOK'S TIP

Use a mezzaluna (a twin-handled curved blade) to chop the herbs, or put them in a large mug and snip them with kitchen scissors.

Chop the coriander and parsley finely. Beat the garlic, herbs, ground coriander and butter in a bowl with a wooden spoon, then stir in the breadcrumbs and ground black pepper. Preheat the grill.

Spoon a little of the mixture on to each mussel. Arrange the mussels in a grill pan, using crumpled foil to keep them upright, if necessary. Grill for 2 minutes. Serve garnished with chopped coriander or parsley.

HOT CORIANDER PRAWNS

Don't stint on the coriander when making this hot and spicy starter. Added at the last minute, it retains its flavour and colour better.

Serves 4–6

1 garlic clove, crushed

1cm/½in piece of fresh root ginger, peeled and chopped

1 small fresh red chilli, seeded and chopped

10ml/2 tsp sugar

15ml/1 tbsp light soy sauce

15ml/1 tbsp vegetable oil

5ml/1 tsp sesame oil

juice of 1 lime

salt, to taste

675g/1½lb whole raw prawns

175g/6oz/1 cup cherry tomatoes

½ cucumber, cut into chunks

1 small bunch of coriander, roughly chopped

Combine the garlic, ginger, chilli and sugar in a mortar and pound to a paste with a pestle. Add the soy sauce, vegetable and sesame oils, lime juice and salt. Arrange the prawns in a single layer in a shallow dish, pour over the marinade and coat well. Cover and marinate for as long as possible, preferably 8 hours.

Preheat the grill. Drain the prawns and thread them on to bamboo skewers, alternately with the tomatoes and cucumber. Grill for 3–4 minutes, brushing occasionally with any remaining marinade. Transfer to a platter, scatter with the coriander and serve.

Avocado, Coriander and Fish Salad

Avocado and smoked fish make a good combination, especially when flavoured with coriander and spices.

Serves 4

15g/½oz/1 tbsp butter or margarine

½ onion, finely sliced

5ml/1 tsp mustard seeds

225g/8oz smoked mackerel, skinned and flaked

30ml/2 tbsp chopped fresh coriander

2 firm tomatoes, peeled and chopped

15ml/1 tbsp lemon juice

For the salad

2 avocados

½ cucumber

15ml/1 tbsp lemon juice

2 firm tomatoes

1 green chilli

salt and ground black pepper

Melt the butter or margarine in a frying pan, add the onion and mustard seeds and fry for about 5 minutes until the onion is soft. Add the fish, chopped coriander, tomatoes and lemon juice and cook over a low heat for 2–3 minutes. Remove from the heat and cool.

Make the salad. Cut the avocados in half and remove the stones and peel. Slice the avocados and cucumber thinly. Place together in a bowl and sprinkle with the lemon juice. Slice the tomatoes. Chop the chilli finely, discarding the seeds.

Spoon the fish mixture on to the centre of a serving plate. Arrange the avocados, cucumber and tomatoes decoratively around the outside of the fish. Alternatively, spoon a quarter of the fish mixture on to each of four serving plates and divide the avocados, cucumber and tomatoes equally among them. Sprinkle with the chopped chilli and a little salt and pepper and serve.

VARIATION

Smoked haddock or cod are good in this salad, or use mackerel and haddock.

CHERRY TOMATOES WITH GUACAMOLE AND CORIANDER

Cherry tomatoes stuffed with a creamy coriander-flavoured guacamole make perfect nibbles.

Makes 24

24 cherry tomatoes

1 large ripe avocado

50g/2oz/¼ cup cream cheese

3–4 dashes of Tabasco sauce, or
* to taste*

grated rind and juice of ½ lime

30ml/2 tbsp chopped fresh coriander

salt

COOK'S TIP

The tomatoes can be prepared the day before. Store in the fridge, ready for filling, upside down in a covered tub. Don't be tempted to make the guacamole ahead of time, though, as it may discolour.

Cut a slice from the bottom of each tomato, then use the handle of a small spoon to scoop out the seeds. Sprinkle the cavities with salt. Drain the tomatoes upside down on kitchen paper for at least 30 minutes.

Cut the avocado in half and discard the stone. Scoop the flesh into a food processor or blender and add the cream cheese. Process until very smooth, scraping down the sides of the bowl once or twice. Season with salt and Tabasco sauce, then add the lime rind and juice. Toss in half of the chopped coriander and process to blend.

Spoon the mixture into a piping bag fitted with a medium star nozzle. Pipe swirls into the tomatoes. Arrange on a platter, sprinkle with the remaining coriander and serve.

FALAFEL

A typical snack food in Israel, crispy falafel seasoned with fresh coriander are served in warm pitta bread.

Serves 4

225g/8oz/1¼ cups dried chick-peas

3 garlic cloves, crushed

5ml/1 tsp cumin seeds

5ml/1 tsp coriander seeds

1 handful of fresh coriander,
    finely chopped

1 handful of flat leaf parsley,
    finely chopped

5ml/1 tsp salt

1.5ml/¼ tsp chilli powder

15ml/1 tbsp lemon juice

5ml/1 tsp baking powder

oil, for deep frying

ground black pepper

pitta bread and hummus, to serve

Soak the chick-peas overnight in water to cover. Drain thoroughly and tip into a saucepan. Add fresh water to cover and bring to the boil. Cook until the chick-peas are soft – this can take anything from 1½ to 4 hours. Drain the chick-peas and put them in a food processor or blender.

Using a pestle, grind the garlic with the cumin and coriander seeds in a mortar. Process the chick-peas until they are broken up. Add the garlic paste, fresh herbs, salt and chilli powder. Process until smooth.

Add the lemon juice, taste for seasoning and add ground pepper or more spice to taste. Scrape into a bowl and leave to stand for about 30 minutes.

Stir in the baking powder and form the mixture into small balls. Fry in hot oil for 2–3 minutes or until the falafel are golden. Drain and serve with pitta bread and hummus.

Fish and Seafood

With its intensely exotic aroma, coriander is
delicious with fish and seafood, particularly
when combined with the clean, bright, astringent
flavours of other aromatics such as limes, chillies,
ginger and lemon grass.

BAKED TUNA WITH CORIANDER CRUST

There's nothing like a fresh coriander marinade to liven up the flavour of meaty fresh tuna steaks.

Serves 4

finely grated rind of 1 lemon
5ml/1 tsp black peppercorns
½ small onion, finely chopped
30ml/2 tbsp chopped fresh coriander
4 fresh tuna steaks, about
*   175g/6oz each*
120ml/4fl oz/½ cup olive oil

For the salsa

1 mango, peeled and diced
finely grated rind and juice of 1 lime
½ fresh red chilli, seeded and
*   finely chopped*

COOK'S TIP

Tuna is an excellent choice for the barbecue. Cook the steaks in a hinged grill over moderately hot coals.

Make the salsa. Mix the mango, lime rind and juice and chilli in a bowl and leave to marinate for at least 1 hour.

Grind the lemon rind, black peppercorns, onion and coriander to a coarse paste, using a mortar and pestle or a coffee grinder. Spoon a quarter of the mixture on to one side of each tuna steak, pressing on well.

Heat the olive oil in a heavy-based frying pan until it begins to smoke. Add the tuna, paste-side down, and fry until a crust forms. Lower the heat and turn the steaks to cook for 1 minute more. Pat off any excess oil with kitchen paper and serve with the salsa.

Thai Fish Salad with Coriander

Treat yourself to this fish salad with its tantalizing mixture of coriander, coconut and chilli flavours.

Serves 4

350g/12oz fillet of red mullet
1 bag mixed salad leaves
½ cucumber
1 papaya, peeled and sliced
1 mango, peeled and sliced
1 large ripe tomato, cut into wedges
3 spring onions, sliced

For the marinade

5ml/1 tsp coriander seeds
5ml/1 tsp fennel seeds
2.5ml/½ tsp cumin seeds
5ml/1 tsp caster sugar
2.5ml/½ tsp hot chilli sauce
30ml/2 tbsp garlic oil
salt

For the dressing

15ml/1 tbsp creamed coconut
60ml/4 tbsp groundnut oil
finely grated rind and juice of 1 lime
1 red chilli, seeded and chopped
5ml/1 tsp granulated sugar
45ml/3 tbsp chopped fresh coriander

Cut the fish into even strips and place in a single layer in a shallow dish. Make the marinade. Put the coriander, fennel and cumin seeds in a mortar. Add the sugar and crush well. Stir in the chilli sauce, garlic oil and salt. Spread the marinade over the fish, cover and leave to stand in a cool place for at least 20 minutes – longer if you have time.

Make the dressing. Place the creamed coconut in a screw-top jar with 45ml/3 tbsp boiling water and a pinch of salt. Stir until dissolved. Add the oil, lime rind and juice, chilli, sugar and chopped fresh coriander. Close the jar tightly, shake well to mix and set aside.

Wash and spin the salad leaves. Peel and cut the cucumber into batons. Place them in a bowl and add the papaya, mango, tomato and spring onions. Pour over the dressing, toss well, then distribute among four large plates.

Heat a large non-stick frying pan, add the fish and cook for 5 minutes, turning once. Arrange the cooked fish on the salad and serve.

CORIANDER-MARINATED FISH STEAKS

Ground and fresh coriander combine to make a marinade and a sauce for succulent fish steaks.

Serves 4

4 halibut or cod steaks or cutlets,
    about 175g/6oz each
juice of 1 lemon
1 garlic clove, crushed
5ml/1 tsp paprika
5ml/1 tsp ground coriander
2.5ml/½ tsp dried tarragon
plain flour, for dusting
60ml/4 tbsp olive oil, plus extra for
    frying onion
300ml/½ pint/1¼ cups fish stock
2 red chillies, seeded and
    finely chopped
30ml/2 tbsp chopped fresh coriander
1 red onion, sliced into rings
salt and ground black pepper

Place the fish in a single layer in a shallow dish. Mix the lemon juice, garlic, paprika, ground coriander, tarragon and a little salt and pepper in a bowl. Spoon the mixture over the fish, cover loosely with clear film and marinate for a few hours, or overnight, in the fridge.

Dust the fish with flour. Gently heat the oil in a large non-stick frying pan. Fry the fish for a few minutes on each side, until golden brown all over, then pour the fish stock into the pan. Cover and simmer for about 5 minutes until the fish is thoroughly cooked.

Add the chillies and half the chopped coriander to the pan. Simmer for 5 minutes more, then transfer the fish and sauce to a serving plate. Keep it hot.

Wipe the pan, heat some oil and stir-fry the onion until speckled brown. Scatter the remaining chopped coriander over the fish, and serve.

SALMON WITH SIZZLING CORIANDER

This superb salmon dish comes from America, where fresh coriander is known as "cilantro".

Serves 4

4 salmon steaks, about
175g/6oz each
60ml/4 tbsp chopped fresh coriander
45ml/3 tbsp grated fresh root ginger
3 spring onions, finely chopped
60ml/4 tbsp soy sauce, plus extra
to serve
75ml/5 tbsp olive oil
salt and ground black pepper
lettuce and coriander sprigs,
to garnish

Season the salmon steaks on both sides with salt and pepper. Prepare a steamer (see Cook's Tip), add the salmon steaks, cover and steam for 7–8 minutes until the fish is opaque throughout.

Place the steamed salmon steaks on warmed plates. Divide the chopped coriander among them, mounding it on top of the fish. Sprinkle with the ginger and then the spring onions. Drizzle 15ml/1 tbsp of soy sauce over each salmon steak. Heat the oil in a small heavy-based saucepan until very hot. Spoon the hot oil over each salmon steak and serve immediately, with more soy sauce, if you like. Garnish with lettuce and coriander sprigs.

COOK'S TIP
If you do not own a steamer, cook the fish steaks on a lightly buttered plate over a pan of simmering water. Cover the fish with greaseproof paper or invert a second plate on top.

FISH KEBABS WITH CORIANDER

Skewers of fresh fish and vegetables basted in a coriander marinade make irresistible kebabs.

Serves 4

275g/10oz cod fillets, or any other
   firm white fish fillets, skinned

45ml/3 tbsp lemon juice

5ml/1 tsp grated fresh root ginger

2 fresh green chillies, finely chopped

15ml/1 tbsp finely chopped
   fresh coriander

15ml/1 tbsp finely chopped
   fresh mint

5ml/1 tsp ground coriander

5ml/1 tsp salt

1 red pepper

1 green pepper

½ cauliflower

8–10 button mushrooms

8 cherry tomatoes

15ml/1 tbsp soya oil

saffron rice, to serve

Cut the fish fillets into large chunks. Mix the lemon juice, ginger, chillies, fresh coriander, mint, ground coriander and salt in a mixing bowl. Add the fish chunks, mix to coat and marinate for about 30 minutes.

Cut the red and green peppers into large squares, discarding the core and seeds from each. Divide the cauliflower into individual florets. Preheat the grill.

Thread the peppers, cauliflower florets, mushrooms and cherry tomatoes alternately with the fish pieces on to four skewers. Brush the kebabs with the oil and any remaining marinade. Transfer to a flameproof dish and grill for 7–10 minutes, or until the fish is opaque throughout. Serve on a bed of saffron rice.

RED SNAPPER WITH CORIANDER

Mexico is the source of this exciting fish dish. The coriander cooks down with the chillies, onion and pan juices to make a delicious sauce.

Serves 4

*900g/2lb red snapper fillets, or other
    white fish fillets*
90ml/6 tbsp lime or lemon juice
60ml/4 tbsp olive oil
1 onion, finely chopped
*50g/2oz/2 cups fresh coriander,
    finely chopped*
*2 drained canned jalapeño chillies,
    rinsed, seeded and sliced*
salt and ground black pepper
coriander sprigs, to garnish
tomato rice, to serve

Place the fish in a shallow dish. Season with salt and pepper and drizzle the lime or lemon juice over. Cover and set aside for 15 minutes.

Preheat the oven to 180°C/350°F/Gas 4. Heat all but 15ml/1 tbsp of the oil in a frying pan and sauté the onion until soft. Meanwhile, using the reserved oil, thinly coat the bottom of an ovenproof dish which is just large enough to hold the fish fillets in a single layer. Arrange the fish in the dish and pour over any remaining marinating liquid. Top with the sautéed onion and the oil from the pan.

Sprinkle over the coriander and chillies. Bake for 20–25 minutes, or until the fish is opaque throughout. Garnish with coriander sprigs and serve with tomato rice.

PRAWNS AND CORIANDER SALAD

Prawns and coriander help to provide a wonderful balance of colours, textures and flavours in this salad.

Serves 4

1 ripe tomato, peeled

½ iceberg lettuce, shredded

1 small onion, shredded

1 small bunch of fresh
   coriander, shredded

15ml/1 tbsp lemon juice

450g/1lb cooked prawns, peeled
   and deveined

1 Granny Smith apple

salt

For the dressing

75ml/5 tbsp mayonnaise

15ml/1 tbsp mild curry paste

15ml/1 tbsp tomato ketchup

To decorate

8 whole prawns

8 lemon wedges

4 fresh coriander sprigs

Cut the peeled tomato in half, squeeze out all the seeds, then cut the flesh into large dice.

Mix the lettuce, onion and coriander with the tomato, moisten with lemon juice and season with salt.

Make the dressing. Combine the mayonnaise, curry paste and tomato ketchup in a small bowl. Stir in enough water (about 30ml/2 tbsp) to thin the dressing, and season to taste with salt.

Add the cooked prawns to the dressing. Peel the apple and grate it into the mixture. Divide the shredded lettuce mixture among four plates or bowls. Pile the prawn dressing in the centre of each and decorate with two whole prawns, two lemon wedges and a coriander sprig.

CORIANDER-COATED PRAWNS

Taste sensations come thick and fast when you bite into one of these prawns. First, there is golden grilled cheese, then a crisp coriander crust and finally succulent shellfish.

Serves 4

75g/3oz/¾ cup cornflour

5–10ml/1–2 tsp cayenne pepper

2.5ml/½ tsp ground cumin

5ml/1 tsp salt

30ml/2 tbsp chopped fresh coriander

plain flour, for dredging

900g/2lb large raw prawns, peeled and deveined

60ml/4 tbsp vegetable oil

115g/4oz/1 cup grated mature Cheddar cheese

lime wedges and tomato salsa, to serve

COOK'S TIP

When preparing the prawns, remove the heads, but leave the tails intact.

Mix the cornflour, cayenne pepper, cumin, salt and coriander in a bowl. Have ready two shallow bowls, one holding water and the other the flour for dredging.

Coat the prawns lightly in flour, then dip in water and roll in the cornflour mixture to coat.

Heat the oil in a non-stick frying pan. When hot, add the prawns, in batches if necessary. Cook for 2–3 minutes on each side, until they are opaque. Drain on kitchen paper.

Place the prawns in a single layer in a large baking dish, or individual dishes. Sprinkle the cheese evenly over the top. Grill for 2–3 minutes, until the cheese melts. Serve immediately, with lime wedges and a tomato salsa.

CORIANDER CRAB WITH COCONUT

Coriander seeds add a pungent taste to this spicy dish – simply serve it with plain warm naan bread.

Serves 4

40g/1½ oz/½ cup dried unsweetened
   coconut flakes

2 garlic cloves, roughly chopped

5cm/2in piece of fresh root ginger,
   peeled and grated

2.5ml/½ tsp cumin seeds

1 small cinnamon stick, broken

2.5ml/½ tsp ground turmeric

2 dried red chillies, crumbled

15ml/1 tbsp coriander seeds

2.5ml/½ tsp poppy seeds

15ml/1 tbsp vegetable oil

1 onion, sliced

1 small green pepper, cut into strips

16 crab claws

fresh coriander sprigs, crushed,
   to garnish

150ml/¼ pint/⅔ cup natural yogurt,
   to serve

Place the dried coconut, garlic, ginger, cumin seeds, cinnamon, turmeric, chillies, and coriander and poppy seeds in a food processor or blender. Process until well blended.

Heat the oil in a wok and fry the onion until soft, but not coloured. Stir in the green pepper and stir-fry for 1 minute, then remove the vegetables with a slotted spoon. Set aside.

Heat the wok again. Add the crab claws, stir-fry for 2 minutes, then briefly return all the spiced vegetables to the wok. Toss over the heat for about 1 minute. Garnish with fresh coriander sprigs and serve with the cooling natural yogurt.

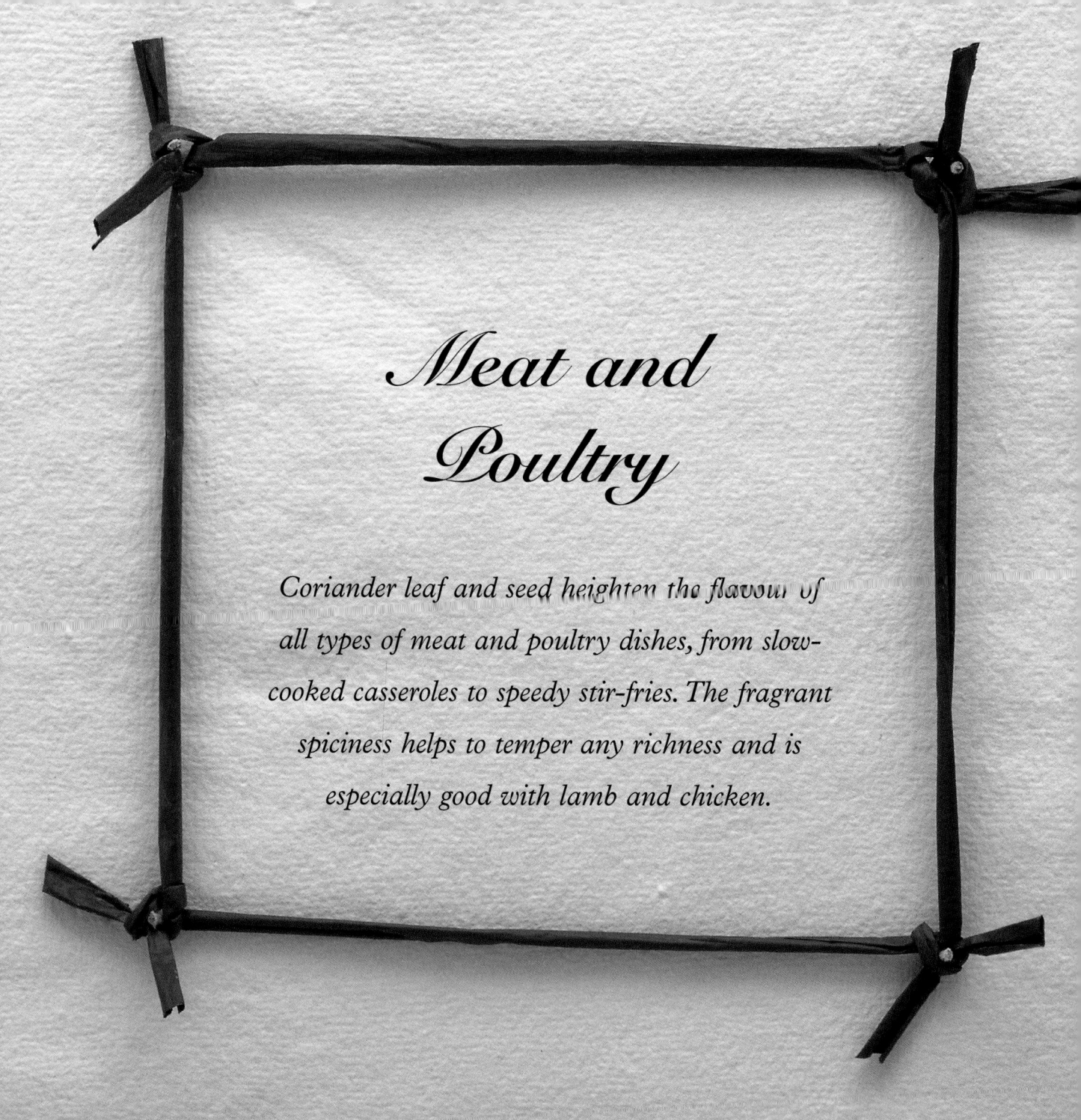

Meat and Poultry

Coriander leaf and seed heighten the flavour of all types of meat and poultry dishes, from slow-cooked casseroles to speedy stir-fries. The fragrant spiciness helps to temper any richness and is especially good with lamb and chicken.

BEEF AND CORIANDER RAGOUT

Based on the ever-popular couscous recipes of North Africa, this coriander-spiced ragoût mixes minced beef with a mixture of fresh vegetables.

Serves 4

15ml/1 tbsp oil

450g/1lb/4 cups minced beef

1 garlic clove, crushed

1 onion, quartered

30ml/2 tbsp plain flour

150ml/¼ pint/⅔ cup dry white wine

150ml/¼ pint/⅔ cup beef stock

2 baby turnips, chopped

115g/4oz swede, chopped

2 carrots, cut into chunks

2 courgettes, cut into chunks

15ml/1 tbsp chopped fresh coriander

5ml/1 tsp ground coriander

225g/8oz/1½ cups couscous

salt and ground black pepper

fresh coriander, to garnish

Heat the oil in a large saucepan. Add the minced beef and fry for 5 minutes, stirring frequently. Add the garlic and onion. Cook for a further 3 minutes, then stir in the flour. Cook for 1 minute. Add the wine and stock and bring to the boil, stirring all the time.

Add the prepared vegetables with the fresh and ground coriander. Stir in salt and pepper to taste. Lower the heat, cover and cook for 15 minutes.

Meanwhile, place the couscous in a bowl. Pour in boiling water to cover. Leave to stand for 10 minutes. Drain and place the couscous in a lined steamer or colander. Remove the lid from the saucepan containing the vegetables and place the steamer on top. Steam the couscous over the pan for 30 minutes more. Garnish with fresh coriander and serve.

SPICY MEATBALLS WITH CORIANDER

Coriander is the traditional flavouring for these tasty Indonesian meatballs.

Makes 24

1 large onion, roughly chopped

1–2 fresh red chillies, seeded
  and chopped

2 garlic cloves, crushed

1cm/½in cube terasi, prepared

15ml/1 tbsp coriander seeds

5ml/1 tsp cumin seeds

450g/1lb/4 cups lean minced beef

10ml/2 tsp dark soy sauce

5ml/1 tsp soft dark brown sugar

juice of ½ lemon

a little beaten egg

oil, for shallow frying

salt and ground black pepper

fresh coriander sprigs, to garnish

COOK'S TIP
Terasi is a pungent shrimp paste, also known as blachan, kapi or ngapi. It should be heated gently before use.

Put the onion, chillies, garlic and terasi in a food processor or blender. Process in bursts; do not overmix or the onion will become too wet and spoil the consistency of the meatballs. Dry fry the coriander and cumin seeds in a preheated frying pan for about 1 minute, to release the aroma. Do not brown. Tip into a mortar and grind with a pestle.

Put the minced beef in a large mixing bowl. Stir in the onion mixture. Add the ground coriander and cumin, soy sauce, sugar and lemon juice. Stir in salt and pepper to taste, bind with a little beaten egg and shape into small, even-size balls.

Chill the meatballs briefly to firm them up, if necessary. Fry them in shallow oil, turning often, until cooked through and browned. This will take 4–5 minutes, depending on their size.

Remove from the pan with a slotted spoon, drain well on kitchen paper and serve, garnished with coriander sprigs.

CHICKEN AND CORIANDER PIZZA

Coriander and chilli are used to flavour mushrooms and chicken for a pizza with a difference.

Serves 3–4

45ml/3 tbsp olive oil

*350g/12oz boneless, skinless chicken
  breasts, cut into thin strips*

1 bunch of spring onions, sliced

1 fresh red chilli, seeded and chopped

*1 red pepper, seeded and cut into
  thin strips*

*75g/3oz fresh shiitake mushrooms,
  wiped and sliced*

*1 pizza base, about 25–30cm/
  10–12in diameter*

15ml/1 tbsp chilli oil

60ml/4 tbsp chopped fresh coriander

150g/5oz mozzarella cheese

salt and ground black pepper

COOK'S TIP

*Use the spicy chicken mixture
as a filling for baked potatoes
or pitta pockets. Or simply pile
it on toasted ciabatta bread.*

Preheat the oven to 220°C/425°F/Gas 7. Heat 30ml/2 tbsp of the olive oil in a wok or large frying pan. Add the chicken, spring onions, chilli, pepper and mushrooms and stir-fry over a high heat for 2–3 minutes until the chicken is firm but still slightly pink inside. Sprinkle over salt and pepper to taste, pour off any excess oil, then set the chicken mixture aside to cool.

Brush the pizza base with chilli oil. Stir the coriander into the chicken mixture, spoon it over the pizza and drizzle over the remaining olive oil.

Grate the mozzarella cheese and sprinkle it over the pizza. Bake for 15–20 minutes until the crust is crisp and golden. Serve immediately.

SPICY CORIANDER CHICKEN

Chicken thighs basted in a spicy coriander marinade are perfect for parties or lively midweek meals.

Serves 6

12 chicken thighs
90ml/6 tbsp lemon juice
5ml/1 tsp grated fresh root ginger
2 garlic cloves, crushed
2 dried red chillies, crumbled
5ml/1 tsp salt
5ml/1 tsp soft light brown sugar
30ml/2 tbsp clear honey
30ml/2 tbsp chopped fresh coriander
1 fresh green chilli, finely chopped
30ml/2 tbsp vegetable oil
fresh coriander sprigs, to garnish

COOK'S TIP
Adjust the quantity of dried chillies to suit the diners. Remove the seeds if a milder flavour is preferred.

Prick the chicken thighs with a fork, rinse, pat dry and set aside in a bowl. Mix the lemon juice, ginger, garlic, crumbled dried red chillies, salt, sugar and honey in a large mixing bowl. Add the chicken thighs and coat well. Cover and set aside for about 45 minutes.

Preheat the grill. Add the fresh coriander and chopped green chilli to the chicken thigh mixture, then arrange the thighs in a flameproof dish. Pour over any remaining marinade, then baste with the oil, using a pastry brush.

Grill the chicken thighs for 15–20 minutes, turning and basting occasionally, until cooked through and browned. Transfer to a serving dish, garnish with the fresh coriander sprigs and serve.

Stir-fried Coriander Chicken

This satisfying stir-fry, flavoured with fresh coriander, is perfect for a speedy supper or lunch.

Serves 4

275g/10oz Chinese egg noodles

30ml/2 tbsp vegetable oil

3 spring onions, chopped

1 garlic clove, crushed

2.5cm/1in piece of fresh root
  ginger, grated

5ml/1 tsp hot paprika

5ml/1 tsp ground coriander

3 skinless, boneless chicken
  breasts, sliced

115g/4oz/1 cup sugar-snap peas,
  topped and tailed

115g/4oz baby sweetcorn, halved

225g/8oz/1 cup fresh beansprouts

15ml/1 tbsp cornflour

45ml/3 tbsp soy sauce

45ml/3 tbsp lemon juice

15ml/1 tbsp granulated sugar

45ml/3 tbsp chopped fresh coriander,
  to garnish

Bring a large saucepan of salted water to the boil. Add the noodles and cook according to the packet instructions. Drain, cover and keep warm.

Heat the oil in a wok or large heavy-based frying pan. Add the spring onions and cook over a gentle heat. Mix in the garlic, ginger, paprika, ground coriander and chicken, then stir-fry for 3–4 minutes. Add the sugar-snap peas, sweetcorn and beansprouts and steam briefly. Add the noodles and toss over the heat.

Combine the cornflour, soy sauce, lemon juice and sugar in a small bowl. Add to the wok or pan and simmer briefly to thicken. Serve garnished with chopped coriander.

LAMB AND CORIANDER FILO PIE

Crisp golden filo contrasts with a fruity lamb filling that is lightly spiced with coriander and cumin.

Serves 4

15ml/1 tbsp oil

450g/1lb/4 cups minced lamb

1 red onion, sliced

30ml/2 tbsp chopped fresh coriander

30ml/2 tbsp plain flour

300ml/½ pint/1¼ cups lamb stock

*50g/2oz/½ cup drained canned
   chick-peas*

5ml/1 tsp ground cumin

225g/8oz filo pastry

25g/1oz/2 tbsp butter, melted

*115g/4oz/½ cup ready-to-eat
   dried apricots*

1 courgette, sliced

salt and ground black pepper

freshly cooked vegetables, to serve

COOK'S TIP
*Cover any filo sheets not being
used with clear film as the
pastry dries out very rapidly.*

Preheat the oven to 190°C/375°F/Gas 5. Heat the oil in a large pan. Add the minced lamb and cook for 5 minutes. Stir in the onion, fresh coriander and flour and cook for 1 minute more.

Pour in the stock and chick-peas. Add salt and pepper to taste and stir in the cumin. Cook for 20 minutes, stirring occasionally.

Line a deep ovenproof dish with four sheets of filo pastry, brushing each sheet lightly with melted butter as it is placed in the dish. Spoon in the mince mixture. Top with dried apricots and courgette slices.

Lay two sheets of filo pastry on top of the filling and brush with melted butter. Fold or scrunch the remaining sheets on top. Pour on the remainder of the butter and bake for 40 minutes. Serve immediately with a selection of freshly cooked vegetables.

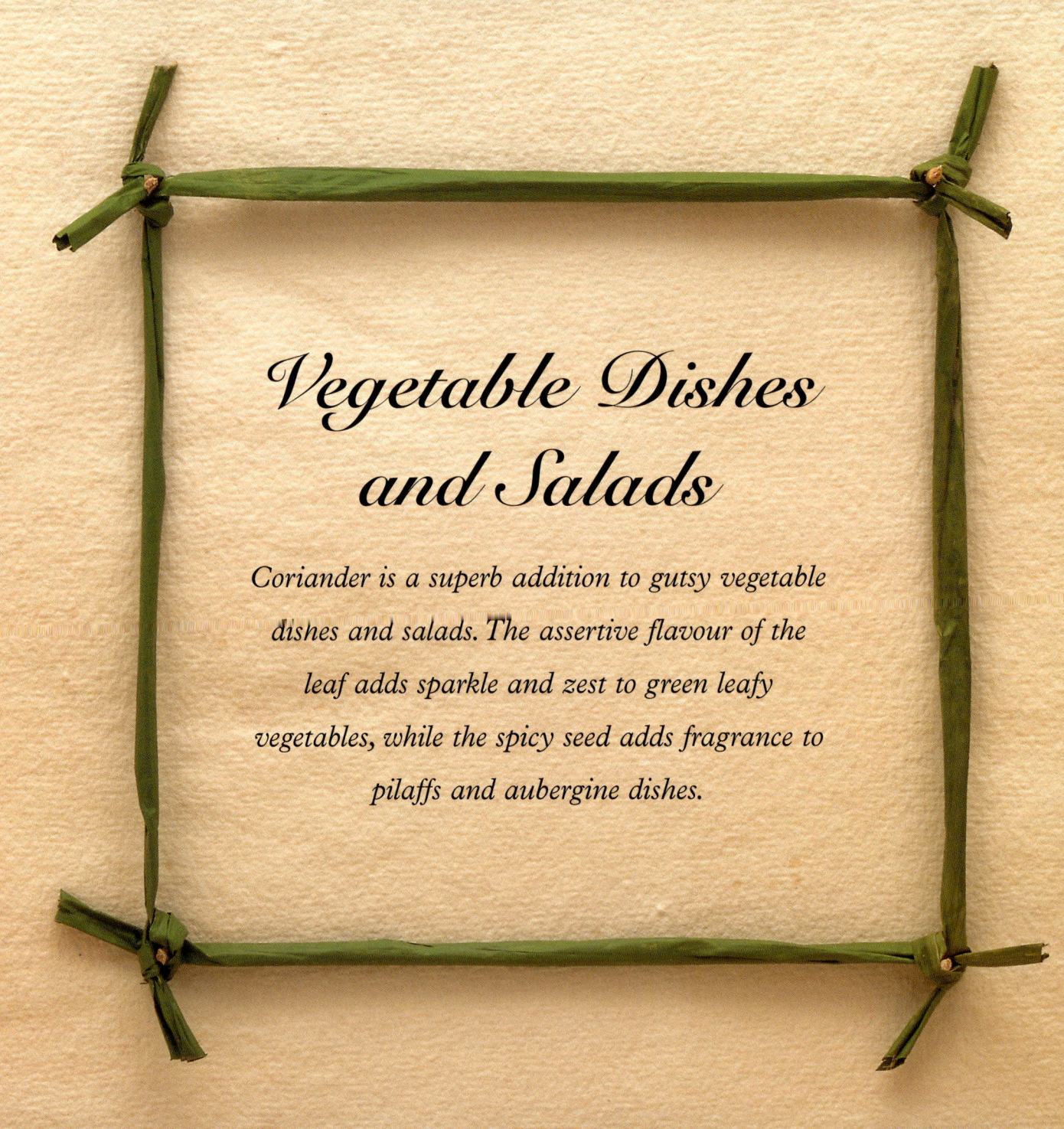

Vegetable Dishes and Salads

Coriander is a superb addition to gutsy vegetable dishes and salads. The assertive flavour of the leaf adds sparkle and zest to green leafy vegetables, while the spicy seed adds fragrance to pilaffs and aubergine dishes.

CARROT AND CORIANDER SOUFFLES

Depending on how it is used, coriander can give a robust or a delicate flavour. Here, it perfectly complements carrots in these light-as-air soufflés.

Serves 4
450g/1lb young carrots
30ml/2 tbsp chopped fresh coriander
4 eggs, separated
salt and ground black pepper

Peel the carrots, but do not slice them. Bring a saucepan of lightly salted water to the boil. Add the carrots and cook for 20 minutes or until tender. Drain, and process until smooth in a food processor or blender.

Preheat the oven to 200°C/400°F/Gas 6. Grease four individual ramekins. Season the puréed carrots well, and stir in the chopped coriander. Fold in the egg yolks.

In a separate bowl, whisk the egg whites until stiff. Fold the egg whites into the carrot mixture and pour into the prepared ramekins. Bake for about 20 minutes, or until the soufflés are risen and golden. Serve immediately.

BEAN AND CORIANDER SALAD

A coriander dressing poured over wholesome beans makes a healthy and extremely tasty salad.

Serves 4

275g/10oz/1½ cups dried pinto
   beans, soaked and drained

1 bay leaf

45ml/3 tbsp coarse salt

2 ripe tomatoes, diced

4 spring onions, finely chopped

For the dressing

60ml/4 tbsp fresh lemon juice

90ml/6 tbsp olive oil

1 garlic clove, crushed

45ml/3 tbsp chopped fresh coriander

salt and ground black pepper

coriander sprig, to garnish

VARIATION

*For a quick and easy salad, use
a drained 425g/15oz can of
chick-peas or butter beans. Just
simmer for a few minutes with
the bay leaf before using.*

Put the pinto beans in a large saucepan. Add fresh cold water to cover and the bay leaf. Bring to the boil, then lower the heat, cover and simmer for 30 minutes. Add the salt and simmer for 30 minutes, or until the beans are tender. Drain, discarding the bay leaf. Set aside to cool slightly.

Make the dressing. In a bowl, mix the lemon juice and 5ml/1 tsp salt until dissolved. Gradually whisk in the oil until the dressing is thick. Add the garlic and coriander, with pepper to taste.

While the beans are still warm, place them in a large bowl. Add the dressing and toss to coat. Leave the beans to cool completely.

Add the tomatoes and spring onions and toss to coat evenly. Allow the salad to stand for at least 30 minutes before serving, garnished with a coriander sprig.

NUT AND CORIANDER PILAFF

Ground coriander adds fragrance to basmati rice in this perfect pilaff.

Serves 4–6

225g/8oz/1 cup basmati rice

15–30ml/1–2 tbsp sunflower oil

1 onion, chopped

1 garlic clove, crushed

1 large carrot, coarsely grated

5ml/1 tsp cumin seeds

10ml/2 tsp black mustard
  seeds (optional)

10ml/2 tsp ground coriander

4 cardamom pods

475ml/16fl oz/2 cups vegetable
  stock or water

1 bay leaf

75g/3oz/¾ cup unsalted nuts

salt and ground black pepper

fresh chopped coriander, to garnish

Put the rice into a large bowl of cold water. Swill the grains around with your hands, then tip out the cloudy water. Repeat this action about five times. If there is time, soak the rice for 30 minutes, then drain well in a sieve.

Heat the oil in a large shallow pan. Fry the onion, garlic and carrot over a gentle heat for a few minutes, then stir in the rice, seeds and spices. Cook for about 1–2 minutes, stirring, so that the grains are all coated in the oil.

Pour in the stock, add the bay leaf and season well. Bring to the boil, lower the heat, cover and simmer gently for 10 minutes. Without lifting the lid, remove the pan from the heat and leave for 5 minutes; this helps the rice to firm up and finish cooking. When the rice is fully cooked, there will be small steam holes in the centre. Discard the bay leaf and cardamom pods.

Stir in the nuts and check the seasoning. Scatter the chopped coriander over the pilaff and serve at once.

FRAGRANT CORIANDER RICE

A soft, fluffy rice dish, perfumed with fresh lemon grass and flavoured with coriander.

Serves 4

225g/8oz/1 cup brown basmati rice

15ml/1 tbsp olive oil

1 onion, chopped

2.5cm/1in piece of fresh root ginger,
*   peeled and finely chopped*

7.5ml/1½ tsp coriander seeds

7.5ml/1½ tsp cumin seeds

1 piece of lemon grass, finely chopped

grated rind of 2 limes

750ml/1¼ pints/3 cups
*   vegetable stock*

60ml/4 tbsp chopped fresh coriander

lime wedges, to serve

> **COOK'S TIP**
>
> *Other varieties of rice, such as white basmati or long grain, can be used for this dish, but you will need to adjust the cooking times accordingly.*

Put the rice into a large bowl of cold water. Swill the grains around with your hands, then tip out the cloudy water (the rice will quickly sink to the bottom). Repeat this action about five times. If there is time, soak the rice for about 5 minutes.

Heat the oil in a large saucepan and add the onion, spices, lemon grass and grated lime rind. Cook gently for 2–3 minutes.

Add the rice, turning it in the mixture to coat the grains. Cook for 1 minute more, then add the stock and bring to the boil. Reduce the heat to very low and cover the pan. Cook gently for 30 minutes, then check the rice; if it is still crunchy, cover the pan again and leave for a further 3–5 minutes. Remove from the heat.

Stir in the fresh coriander, fluff up the grains, cover the pan and leave for 10 minutes. Serve at once, with lime wedges.

CORIANDER AND VEGETABLE STEW

Coriander is used in combination with chick-peas and aubergine in this spicy West African stew.

Serves 3–4

45ml/3 tbsp olive oil

1 red onion, chopped

3 garlic cloves, crushed

115g/4oz sweet potatoes, peeled and diced

1 large aubergine, diced

425g/15oz can chick-peas, drained

5ml/1 tsp dried tarragon

2.5ml/½ tsp dried thyme

5ml/1 tsp ground cumin

5ml/1 tsp ground turmeric

2.5ml/½ tsp ground allspice

5 drained canned plum tomatoes, chopped, plus 60ml/4 tbsp of the can juices

6 ready-to-eat dried apricots

600ml/1 pint/2½ cups vegetable stock

1 fresh green chilli, seeded and finely chopped

30ml/2 tbsp chopped fresh coriander

salt and ground black pepper

Heat the olive oil in a large saucepan over a medium heat. Add the onion, garlic and sweet potatoes and cook for about 5 minutes until the onion has softened slightly.

Stir in the diced aubergine, then add the chick-peas and the herbs and spices. Stir well to mix and cook over a gentle heat for a few minutes.

Add the tomatoes and the reserved juice from the can, with the apricots, stock and chilli. Stir in salt and pepper to taste. Bring slowly to the boil and cook for about 15 minutes, or until the sweet potatoes are tender. Add the fresh coriander, stir and adjust the seasoning if necessary. Serve at once.

PLANTAIN AND BANANA SALAD WITH CORIANDER SAUCE

The plantains and bananas are cooked in their skins to retain their soft texture. This helps them to absorb the full flavour of the coriander dressing.

Serves 4

2 firm yellow plantains

3 green bananas

1 garlic clove, crushed

1 red onion, halved and thinly sliced

30ml/2 tbsp chopped fresh coriander

45ml/3 tbsp sunflower oil

20ml/4 tsp malt vinegar

salt and ground black pepper

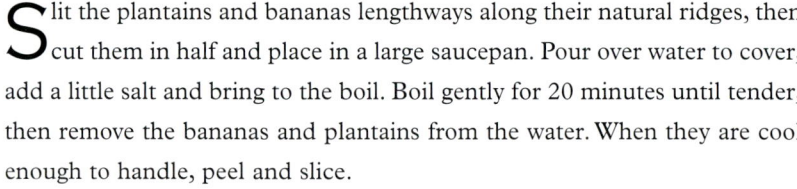

Slit the plantains and bananas lengthways along their natural ridges, then cut them in half and place in a large saucepan. Pour over water to cover, add a little salt and bring to the boil. Boil gently for 20 minutes until tender, then remove the bananas and plantains from the water. When they are cool enough to handle, peel and slice.

Put the plantain and banana slices into a bowl and add the garlic and onion. Mix well.

Add the coriander, oil and vinegar, with salt and pepper to taste. Toss together to mix, then serve as an accompaniment to a main dish, such as Spicy Coriander Chicken.

WARM CHICKEN SALAD WITH SESAME AND CORIANDER DRESSING

Serving this salad warm makes the most of the wonderful sesame and coriander flavourings.

Serves 6

4 skinless, boneless chicken breasts

225g/8oz/2 cups mangetouts

2 heads decorative lettuce, such as
    lollo rosso or feuille de chêne, torn
    into pieces

3 carrots, peeled and cut into
    small matchsticks

175g/6oz/2¼ cups button
    mushrooms, sliced

5 rindless smoked streaky
    bacon rashers

15ml/1 tbsp chopped fresh coriander,
    to garnish

salt

For the dressing

120ml/4fl oz/½ cup lemon juice

30ml/2 tbsp wholegrain mustard

250ml/8fl oz/1 cup olive oil

75ml/5 tbsp sesame oil

5ml/1 tsp coriander seeds, crushed

Mix the dressing ingredients. Place the chicken breasts in a dish and pour on half of the dressing. Cover and marinate overnight in the fridge.

Bring a pan of lightly salted water to the boil. Add the mangetouts and cook for 2 minutes. Drain, refresh under cold water and drain again.

Mix the lettuce, mangetouts, carrots and mushrooms in a bowl. Toss to mix, then divide among six individual dishes. Preheat the grill.

Arrange the chicken breasts on the grill rack and grill for 8–10 minutes until cooked through. Meanwhile, heat the bacon in a dry frying pan until the fat runs, then fry until crisp.

Slice the chicken thinly and arrange on the salads. Crumble the bacon on top. Add the reserved dressing to the fat in the pan and heat briefly. Pour a little dressing over each salad, garnish with fresh coriander and serve.

BEANSPROUTS WITH CORIANDER

This simple, delicious dish is given extra zest by the addition of fresh coriander. For the freshest results, sprout your own beans.

Serves 3–4

*30ml/2 tbsp sunflower or
   groundnut oil*
225g/8oz beansprouts
2 spring onions, chopped
1 garlic clove, crushed
30ml/2 tbsp soy sauce
10ml/2 tsp sesame oil
15ml/1 tbsp sesame seeds
30ml/2 tbsp chopped fresh coriander
salt and ground black pepper

COOK'S TIP

You can buy beans for sprouting from most health food shops. Follow the directions on the packet to produce your own sprouts for this stir-fry. Beansprouts can be stored in the fridge for up to two days.

Heat the oil in a large wok and stir-fry the beansprouts, spring onions and garlic for 3–5 minutes.

Add the soy sauce, sesame oil, sesame seeds and chopped coriander, with plenty of salt and pepper to taste. Toss over the heat for 1–2 minutes more and serve.

AVOCADO AND CORIANDER SALAD DIP

A bowl of this creamy coriander dip is wonderful with crudités, tortilla chips and crispy potato skins.

Serves 4

2 large ripe avocados

2 garlic cloves, crushed

1 small onion, finely chopped

60ml/4 tbsp lemon juice

1 fresh green chilli, seeded and
*   chopped (optional)*

45ml/3 tbsp chopped fresh coriander

salt

Tabasco sauce, to taste

To serve

5 large potatoes

15ml/1 tbsp vegetable oil

4 celery sticks, cut into fingers

3 large ripe tomatoes, cut into wedges

1 mild Spanish onion, cut into strips

tortilla chips

Cut the avocados in half, lengthways, discard the stones and scoop the flesh into a food processor or blender. Add the garlic, onion, lemon juice and chopped green chilli, if using. Process roughly. Add the coriander, and season to taste with salt and Tabasco sauce. Cover tightly with clear film to prevent discoloration.

Prepare the potato skins. Peel the potatoes thickly, aiming for 6–8 large pieces of peel from each one. Place the skins in a saucepan, pour in boiling water to cover and cook for 5 minutes. Preheat the grill. Drain the potato skins well, toss them in oil, season with salt and grill them until crisp.

Turn the avocado dip out into an attractive bowl. Serve with the potato skins, crudités and tortilla chips.

CURRIED CORIANDER AND PARSNIP PIE

Sweet, creamy parsnips are beautifully complemented by the addition of coriander and cheese. This unusual but delicious combination of flavours makes for a very tasty pie.

Serves 4

115g/4oz/1 cup plain flour

115g/4oz/½ cup butter

1 egg yolk, beaten with 10ml/
   2 tsp water

salt and ground black pepper

For the filling

8 shallots, peeled

2 large parsnips, thinly sliced

2 carrots, thinly sliced

25g/1oz/2 tbsp butter or margarine

30ml/2 tbsp wholemeal flour

15ml/1 tbsp mild curry or
   tikka paste

300ml/½ pint/1¼ cups milk

115g/4oz/1 cup grated mature cheese

45ml/3 tbsp chopped fresh coriander

Put the flour in a mixing bowl. Add plenty of salt and pepper, then rub in the butter until the mixture resembles breadcrumbs. Add just enough water to bind the dough, then wrap it in clear film and set it aside in a cool place while you make the filling.

Put the shallots, parsnips and carrots in a saucepan with just enough water to cover. Bring to the boil and blanch the vegetables for 5 minutes. Drain, reserving about 300ml/½ pint/1¼ cups of the liquid.

Melt the butter in a clean pan. Stir in the flour and curry or tikka paste. Cook for 1 minute, then gradually whisk in the reserved stock and milk until smooth. Bring to the boil, stirring constantly, then lower the heat and simmer for 1–2 minutes. Take the pan off the heat, stir in the cheese and seasoning, then mix into the vegetables with the coriander. Pour into a pie dish, and place a pie funnel in the centre. Allow to cool.

Preheat the oven to 200°C/400°F/Gas 6. Roll out the pastry to a round large enough to fit the top of the pie dish. Re-roll the trimmings into long strips. Brush the pastry edges with egg yolk wash and fit the pastry strips on the edge of the dish. Brush again with egg yolk wash, then fit the lid over the funnel. Cut off the overhanging pastry and crimp the edges. Cut a hole for the funnel, brush with the remaining egg yolk wash and make decorations with the trimmings, glazing them too. Bake for 25–30 minutes until the pie crust is golden brown and crisp. Serve immediately.

CHARGRILLED VEGETABLES WITH CORIANDER SALSA

Enjoy a barbecue with these chunky chargrilled vegetables served hot with a no-cook coriander salsa.

Serves 4

1 large sweet potato, cut in
   thick slices
2 courgettes, halved lengthways
2 red peppers, quartered
olive oil, for brushing

For the salsa

2 large tomatoes, peeled and
   finely chopped
2 spring onions, finely chopped
1 small green chilli, chopped
juice of 1 small lime
30ml/2 tbsp chopped fresh coriander
salt and ground black pepper

Bring a small saucepan of lightly salted water to the boil. Add the sweet potato and parboil for 5 minutes until it is barely tender. Drain and leave to cool.

Place the courgettes in a colander. Sprinkle with a little salt and leave to drain for 20 minutes, then rinse and pat dry.

Make the salsa by mixing all the ingredients together in a bowl. Cover and set aside for 30–45 minutes to allow the flavours to blend.

Meanwhile, light the barbecue or preheat the grill. Put the sweet potato slices, courgettes and peppers on the grid or in a hinged basket and brush them with oil. Cook them until they are lightly charred and softened, brushing with oil again and turning at least once. Serve hot with the salsa.

TOMATO AND CORIANDER SALAD RELISH

There are many versions of this coriander relish, which is the traditional accompaniment for an Indian curry. This one will leave your mouth feeling cool and fresh.

Serves 4

3 ripe tomatoes

2 spring onions, chopped

1.5ml/¼ tsp caster sugar

salt

45ml/3 tbsp chopped fresh coriander

Remove the tough cores from the tomatoes with a small knife. Cut them in half, remove the seeds and dice the flesh. Tip the tomatoes into a bowl and add the spring onions, sugar, salt and chopped coriander. Mix well, cover and set aside for at least 30 minutes to allow the flavours to blend. Serve at room temperature.

COOK'S TIP
This salad relish also tastes wonderful with fresh crab, lobster or shellfish.

IMAM BAYILDI

This classic aubergine dish is accented with both ground and fresh coriander. According to legend, Imam Bayildi means "the Imam fainted", because he was so overcome by this delicious dish.

Serves 4

2 aubergines, halved lengthways

60ml/4 tbsp olive oil, plus extra
  if needed

2 large onions, thinly sliced

2 garlic cloves, crushed

1 green pepper, seeded and sliced

400g/14oz can chopped tomatoes

45ml/3 tbsp granulated sugar

5ml/1 tsp ground coriander

30ml/2 tbsp fresh chopped coriander

salt and ground black pepper

crusty bread, to serve

coriander sprigs, to serve

Using a sharp knife, slash the flesh of the aubergines a few times. Place them in a colander, sprinkle the cut sides with salt and leave for about 30 minutes. Rinse well and pat dry.

Preheat the oven to 190°C/375°F/Gas 5. Heat the oil in a frying pan, add the aubergines, cut-sides down, and fry for 5 minutes. Remove with a slotted spoon or tongs and place in a shallow ovenproof dish. Add the onions, garlic and green pepper to the pan, with extra oil if necessary, and cook for about 10 minutes, until the vegetables have softened. Add the tomatoes, sugar and ground coriander with salt and pepper to taste. Cook for about 5 minutes until the mixture has reduced. Stir in the chopped coriander.

Spoon this mixture on top of the aubergines. Cover and bake for about 30–35 minutes. Cool, then chill. Serve cold with crusty bread, garnished with coriander sprigs.

COOK'S TIP
Imam Bayildi can be served hot. It needs no accompaniment other than a bowl of Greek-style yogurt and some crusty bread or naan.

INDEX